# Sing in the Wind With Love

## By

## Rosemary Regina Challoner Wilkinson

ISBN: 0-7596-6951-1

Library of Congress Control Number: 2002090436

This book is printed on acid free paper.

Front Cover: Collage by Rosemary Wilkinson

1stBooks - rev. 02/15/02

# Preface

Rosemary Wilkinson's lyrical ecstasies may be heard throughout the universe wherever the dominant language English is spoken. Full of beauty, delicate, sensitive, reflective mood reinforced by a boundless faith in the divinity that shapes our ends: her poetry induces us Indians to claim her as a sparkling product of the Oriental East.

**Justice S. Mohan,**
Supreme Court of India Ret.
New Delhi, India

# Dedication

To the World Poets living now and yet to come for indeed poetry from our precious Greek civilization, forward and also, Li Po, Tu Fu, Lao Tze, Basho, Tagore, all beckon us to gather together in memory of what they did back then on both sides of the world and forward until the end of the time. Poetry opens doors to each person born round our globe. Poetry is best heralded by U.S.A. Senator Robert C Byrd who in 1979 wrote: "Before ever there were written essays or novels, and long centuries prior to newspapers, radio, television, there was poetry. The development of poetry has been an almost universal phenomenon. Men and women in every nation, culture, tribe have discovered the deep rewards of putting their feelings, hopes, aspirations into rhythmic verse. Through poetry, shepherds have spoken to kings, courtiers have shared their vision with commoners, and men have addressed their most intimate expressions of adoration to the Deity. Poetry is the primal language of the heart. It uses images that are current in many cultures and that are understood across most national boundaries. Even though men speak in hundreds of different dialects and use literally millions of dissimilar words in their discourse, all men share certain great universal emotions and dreams that are best captured by poetry. Poetry is truly an international medium of communication."

Is this not a beckoning to all nations to exchange poetry revealing their sacred and holy heritage, culture and literary traditions, to unite the world in a new joy and happiness? Real pleasure is to be found in the 'knowing of all nuances of languages in poetry having specific matter.' Readers do look for sincerity, wisdom, and professionalism in poetry. Poetry is the legacy "a moment of history the poet helps the younger generation of all peoples."

Rosemary Regina Challoner Wilkinson
U.S.A.

# Prologue

Wilkinson's works have struck me as enhancing the spiritual level of the human beings with her religious fraternity.  Studying, translating her verses I have walked into the poetical world of this poet who wrote first poem at age 14, mother of four children, using simple language for descriptions plain yet vivid, carefully done and applying some novel figures of speech to make scenery depiction lyrical; writes historical poems comparing beautiful living conditions of past with present readers' reminiscence's, lines are full of imaginations, personifications which can be compared with poems of visiting immortals in history of Chinese literature.  She writes of future stressing poets' duties, calling people to find back the noble spiritual world, serene natural world, caring about whole world; her lines are all God's words, only in her name, where no personal, individual gain or loss is expressed.  She devotes all her feeling to mankind's upliftment.

**Yang Xu**, China
(poet)

# Foreword

Cosmic symphony is played ubiquitous on earth. Thunderbolts pop in skies, waves roar in seas, birds sing in woods, reeds rustle in the wind, streams murmur and poets sing along *con moto*: all playing own instruments melodious and harmonious.

On poetry, the critics are cacophonous telling what, why and how one can write. Never mind the Aristotle's *Poetica*, Horace's *"Art of Poetry* or any masters' nagging advice. The Cosmic symphony has been played long before any of the mortals emerged. One cannot ask Cosmos what, why, how to write songs. All sing solely motivated by divine inspiration.

The theme of poetry can be idiosyncratic and highly specialized as we hear the animal songs; elephants trumpet, lions roar, roosters crow, nightingales warble, crickets chirrup. Milton indignant, raised his voice high against the politicians and clergies, Shelley atheistic, ridiculed the hypocrisy of the social upper class, Pushkin heartrending over the slaves sang bucolic songs. Whitman fighting freedom, removed all barriers of rhymes and metrics, Eliot was sentimental for the ravage of war. Rosemary Wilkinson writes *songs of love* in the 20th century deeply moved by the human tragedies in global wars in the name of righteousness and freedom scorching the Eurasian continent killing and maiming tens of millions of lives. Still some 100 local wars are being fought on the globe with no end being in sight. Most of them are of religious causes; the Arab-Jew war in the god's land, Hindu-Moslem war in Cashmere, Moslem-Christian war in Indonesia continue in terms of zero-sum games.

Rosemary has been leading the World Congress of Poets in the past quarter Century under the catchword of "Peace and Brotherhood" holding an annual meeting in different places of the world like San Francisco, Cairo, Istanbul, Madras, Seoul, Tokyo, Sidney…the world poets gather to become brothers and sisters through poetry for a week reciting poetry in own languages and dining and schmoozing in the breeze. Most poets are smart, talented, keen, some arrogant, aloof and selfish; yet, they all come to relax under the warm feather of the hen bird, Rosemary whose smiles sweet, voice silky, manner divine with no tinge of arrogance of her being born a blue blood of Wales and a citizen of the super power. She writes her poems effortless with beautiful images and profound metaphor striking many chords and some of her 21 books have been translated in 36 different languages.

While the fellow American poets, Dickinson and Whitman never married, Rosemary has been happily married celebrating her golden wedding anniversary a couple of years ago. Her husband Henry is a devoted husband helping Rosemary all along financial or otherwise. Their 4 children are all grown ups leading lives as model citizens. On holidays and birthdays the couple make trips to their children living far away. Rosemary is absolutely dedicated to her family and the poetry society.

After serving some 30 years for the society, she has confessed me recently of her retiring from the society. I felt quite sympathetic but I urged her to stay on keep writing her love songs like the great masters of art; Beethoven composed his greatest *"symphony No. 9"* after he became a complete deaf and Degas painted the great picture *"Four dancers"* after he was completely blinded. The book *"Sing in the wind with love"* will not be her last and her better or best books are sure to follow.

**Kim Unsong**
(scientist/poet)
UPLT77

# INDEX

# CALIFORNIA WINTER SKY

The dark sky is in an angry mood,
As far as you can see,
Displaying once more scene of the sacred rood.
Hurling rains fall upon the earth,
All of nature takes cover.
Then lightning strikes,
My pink camellias bow their heads,
Afraid to open their eyes.
And I am in a meditative mood
Watching through my window
All of nature's melodrama
Lifting my spirits anew.

*1966*

# COMET GLIMPSE

*Once in a great while*
*There comes to an age*
*Burning spirit blazing*
*Truth across a page.*
*Where is it going you ask?*
*No one answers to me*
*Except the sustaining mysterious glow*
*leaving behind a legacy*

*1969*

# HUMAN RIGHTS

We are now in a new era of Time
    Caught up as it were beyond knowledge-fare.
Time spreads as the wind across earthly clime
    The lone human cry does it loudly bare.
It speaks of the young and naked in jail
    And tells of the oppressed by world leaders.
Voices are silenced as the people do fail
    To bring forth truth for innocent bleeders.
There are nations who with tyranny rule:
    The people are silent, they are not free,
Other nations are used as a tool
    While the world stands in watch for all to see.
But the wind sings to the heavens above:
    Join Earth brothers and sisters One through Love.

*1977*

*Rosemary Regina Challoner Wilkinson*

# VIEW FROM MY WINDOW

Outside my pane of glass
  There stands an orange tree
Bending low from her burden
  Of fruit about to be.

The radiant sun gleams down
  To warm her leaves of green
No more wind, no more rain,
  To buffet her trunk unseen.

Now the time has finally come
  And even nature derides
But the proud orange tree
  Standing aloft
Bends low, and nobly abides.

*1966*

# ECHELON OF GEMS

*Keep calm impulsive heart of mine*
*if it but take a full life-time*
*make me worthy of the day I was born*
*all imperfection shorn*
*the while I round a furrowed crown*
*to place among the valid worn.*

*1968*

# ON BEING HUMAN

Rains slant in faces
Snow covers houses
Sands Bake in the sun
Waters crest in waves

Man serves as human
Sorrow is his...
Happiness is his...
His glory is human

To breathe is human
To be rich/poor is human
To love is to be human

To be fulfilled is human
To create is to be human
What else matters—
But being human?

*February 13, 1984*
*11:10 am*

# POET WITHOUT A PEN

What do you do
when a poem is coming about
And you have no pen,
nor paper to write it out?

You recite it over and over—
and burn it in your brain
From the very title,
Down to the last refrain,

Then send it upward to
the stars to remember.
You hope they remember,
You hope they remember.

*March 23, 1986*
*8:44 am*

# Pre-Spring

Waters recede from edges of shores
and sailboats yield to strong winds
While the floods gather afar
to displace the animals
Still bent to eat, not minding it all.

Dark skies rage to uproot
the trees and branches float
Down swollen streams
but the birds feed their young
Eagles flap their wings, owls blink
and the road runner hurries
To the awakening of Spring.

*March 19, 1989*
*9:00 pm*

# SPRING IN THE FOOTHILLS
*(Sierra Nevada Mountains)*

Wild purple lupine blooms regally
all over the mountain hillsides—
Blinding yellow scotch broom
spreads like a wildfire
Over the foothills of the Sierra Nevada
here in Northern California.

Wild red sweet peas burst
forth along curvy roads—
Cones form on tall pines straight up
like soldier candles on splashing green foam
Spring is alive with blooming white dogwood,
pink dogwood—in pollen laden air.

Winter will depart when snow blesses
blooming dogwood once again foretold—
Fulfilling Indian adage of long ago.
never failing—happens every year.

*April 26, 1990*
*8:00 am*

# NO PROBLEM

When all the books have then been read
And all world knowledge stored in head.
When all traveling is behind
Bigotry, prejudice made blind.
With all lies, pride and temper gone
A new resurgent life begun.
Man will stand tall on truth alone
Knowing right from wrong will atone.
The world follows, brothers, nations,
Drawing forth a world-wide patience.
For peace on his earth to begin:
First it must burst forth from within.

*April 15, 1983*
*11:44 am*

# PARCHMENT PRESERVATION

Gradually over the years
I added oil to a lamp,
As chance flashed past, and
Slowly awaited the Good things that come
To those who wait.
In the interim I read the
Tao among the great
Poets, painters, saints,
Bible of History.
I found solace in the Music
of the Psalms.
I no longer heard the jingle
of jade when I
First  heard the growth of trees,
the spatter of rain.
I picked up my pen and wrote.
And sometimes what I write is
so beautiful
I know that it comes not from me,
but through me.
And sometimes it tears my heart
(rolling on and I am running to catch up.)
Only time and paper preserve the moment
as the moment preserved.

*1975*

# CALIFORNIA'S APOLOGY TO NATURE

I apologize to the tall trees in the Sierra
I say I'm sorry to fish in the pure blue ocean,
I beg pardon for all carelessness of man,
Having caused such pain to them.

For the oil spilled into water,
Lands devastated by fire—
I apologize brother Nature—
And ask you forgive my human failure.

*1968*

# SOMETHING LIVES

Something lives in me again as
    it did centuries ago.
Something dwells within my heart,
    inside my brain, like bards of old.

Nowhere else now does it reign
    as in the days when it flourished.
Nowhere else can you find it
    for it was unique, even then.

Who will come to restore it
    and bring forth a spiritual age?
Who will draw every nation
    to the new spirit by the bard?

*June 20, 1983*
*9:35 am*

# EARTH, LET ME TAKE YOUR PULSE

I see your dwarf-man mountains,
Fertile plains mirrored in the sky,
I marvel at your busy highways
Passing onlookers rapidly by.

You are busy nations
Linking each other by hand,
To far away places
Across seas, and desert, and land.

But I feel the spirit within you.
I know the measure of your love;
For I am the soul-searching stars—
Your light—
The sun, and the moon above.

*1971*

# I WANT TO GO BACK

I want to go back
to my youth to smell
the fogged-in trees in Golden Gate Park.

Swaying eucalyptus dripping pines
low junipers tall cedars redwood all alive
among the dewey rhododendron-azaleas.

Let me deep breathe this while looking back
reclaiming summer days tennis racquets,
cycling through poplars to beach roaring ocean.

I want to recall always olfactory days
cherished from my girlhood freedom,
deep breathe them fresh over and over again.

*July 18, 1982*
*8:00 am*

15

# I JUST CAME IN FROM THE GARDEN

Summer days pass swiftly—
Days of lying in the sun,
Deep breathing jasmine and roses.

Watching petunias holding regal heads:
Stately camellias past their bloom
Waiting to be fed for next year.

Among the tall hedge, low greenery,
Glowing fountain and tranquil time
Grows the orange and English walnut trees.

It is a place to study skies
Feel the silence of your soul,
Pray, rest, away from it all.

Where do these days go that we long for in winter
To savor slowly, never to part?
I want to cherish them when the snow falls again.

*August 18, 1982*
*8:30 am*

# PLANET EARTH'S LAMENTATION

Holy of Holies we cry
from Planet Earth—
A tiny speck
in our Universe.
Hear our hearts raised together—
all nations with one voice:
Holy, Holy, Holy!

Lift up our hearts to yours—
close our ranks in brotherhood.
Draw us up to the Galaxies—
lift our minds, souls, all:
Holy, Holy, Holy!

We yearn for your Mighty Presence—
let it all come about.
Purify us for the happening—
make us special among your stars:
Holy, Holy, Holy!

*August 24, 1982*
*7:00 pm*

# OUR HOMELESS
*(untouchables)*

They roam the streets day and night
seeking daily care just to live
For something went wrong and they
have yet to figure out why...

A place to sleep or eat or wash
is what they need or someone
To give some clothes for a change
as all humans do each day

Who will build the shelters to house them
and care for their medical needs
Or talk with them and walk with them
as they trudge the streets alone?

This is the country with abundancy
and know-how and resources.
How did this happen to us...
Are they our untouchables?

*August 2, 1989*

# COME AWAY WITH ME

Come, let us take a journey
Around the seas, oceans, gulfs,
Meet the peoples of the earth
Learn of them, culture unearth.

Let us sit beside them
Share their food and drink
Let us get to know them
And find the burden they share.

Let us take the time to listen
To what it is they need
Let us bend, heed, wager peace
And sit in harmony once more.

The birds sing, the crow flies,
The flowers alike bloom;
Are we not like them
Mirroring nature on planet earth?

*September 14, 1982*
*4:00 pm*

# WHY WRITE POETRY?

Poetry is written
   to draw out <u>the within</u>:
To be in touch <u>with spirit,</u>
   part of physical body
To write each word down
   <u>that lifts</u> from the paper
To keep <u>constant interest</u> alive
   with each word written
To form tightened-up thinking
   for <u>economy of prose</u>
To say what <u>no one else says</u>
   for no one else is you
To bring forth the <u>spiritual</u>
   <u>hidden</u> in your humanness
To uplift others who <u>seek respite</u>
   away from the crowding day
To experience <u>the clean</u> after
   writing a poem
To rise up <u>mentally</u> in a light
   of <u>emotional happiness.</u>

*September 12, 1985*
*9:15 am*

# ONE BLUE DOT

From way out here we behold you
spinning with life and glory
For you were created like the heavens
above us here in space, in hurry.

Only upon you lives life and immortal spirit—
only upon you thrives humankind upward
Towards the Eternal yearned for since
time was set eons ago forward.

O great planet as one small blue dot
give praise for your existence.
Give thanks for your creation
give back each day dignity magnificence.

*October 22, 1990*
*2:00 pm*

# PLEA

Dear God make nations brothers
Who cannot war against each other
Who regard each other in dignity
Supplying jobs plentifully.
Allow your Earth to prosper
Give each nation spiritual
And material gain in balance.
Your Earth is good, good will out...
It will obliterate anything less.
Let it all happen, let it come about.
Give man this leadership...
In each and every nation,
Heal the nations.

*November 11, 1984*
*8:30 am*

# WINTER SOLSTICE STORM

Across the somber sky so dark
Swaying limbs and falling leaves
Fill the air with solitude
Drawing deep passages to surface.

Blow hard you scathing winds
Drop every leaf in your path
For there are others rising
Forming beneath the soil to come forth.

*December 21, 1982*

# WHEN

When the resounding spheres
echo it as far
as sound can be heard

From above the heavens
to the earth below
and formed into word

By the populace on bended knee
and heads bowed low
in reverent awe

Of the blessedness of God
giving blessings to those blessed
who give back blessings of happiness, then,

Then, will come the fullness of TIME.

*December 24, 1994*
*5:00 am*

# BROWN-OUT IN TAIPEI

My hair set and out in the rain
    I go to shop for a thing or two
And as I arrive Asia World complex
    lights go out, doors are locked.
So I stand quiet watching people go by
    and used this time to pray a Memorare
Followed by Ave Marias, many more,
    then the lights come on, doors open
All follow quickly in
    and I remember the occasion given
To be set aside, to pray,
    to meditate on others hurrying by
As I thanked God for this time given to me
    to know how much I need to be aside
To pray, to watch, to be quiet, no matter what.

        8/25/94            5:15 A.M.

# POEM IN TAIPEI

Far from home in Taipei
I come to truly learn
Of culture I treasure
Your poems in my heart burn.

August 26, 1994 8:15 A.M.
(written for TV station interview)

# OIL PAINTINGS OF LINDA HONG (Li-Ying)

With rich blend of reds and blues
    welcoming feast of radiant hues
        splattered between serene greens
we travel the imaginary world
    of gypsies, bridges of peace,
        mysterious kingdoms,
and fountains of youth,
    hailing the environmental
        galaxies, origins of life,
to a new oceanic world
    beckoning us view eruption
        from white messenger of peace thus
awakening new feelings
    through vibrant color,
        cherry blossoms fragrant
in sensation of whirlpool
    and eternal love
        beckoning response to
fresh art, mastery in color,
    figure, varied movement,
        all converging into one joyful heart.

U.S.A. poet/author    November 30, 1994    9:56 P.M.

# IN TIME

In time of Teresa of Avila
Men wore the panty hose.

Today women wear them,
Legs shapely, men to impress.

                    May 14, 1995        6:12 P.M.

# WE FORGIVE

We forgive our enemies, for we are
told that they have yet to know
the love of God, for to forgive and
love our enemies, is to know the
Love of God.

5/25/95          8:55 A.M.

# PEACE OF SPRING

Yellow flowers rise above growing
    new green silently saying
IT IS SPRING

As I pass enroute California
    into Arizona, I reply,
YOU FILL MY HEART

With a peace and calm
I want to own all year long.

               Feb. 29, 1996     1:10 PM

## HIGH CLOUDS

High clouds
    painting the
        mountains black,
always silent
    giving us
        only beauty, peace.

May 29, 1997      12:03 PM

# HEAVEN MET TO SEND A POET

Heaven met to send a poet down
    among the throngs down
        below the heavens:

They looked about
    deciding which one they thought
        would give permission for such
to fill intended purpose they held.

Shall it be one chosen
    from among those with honors,
        success, fulfillment, degrees, or
strong of heart, of much courage?

So finally they fully concluded
    they would choose one noted
        for failure, elevating others
more worthy, more eligible than them all:
a pliable servant, less noted by the world.

February 22, 1998    4 P.M.

# FREEDOMS

First was at first breath we took
    having followed <u>gift of LIFE</u> from God.
Second was learning from within
    the difference of right and wrong.
To breathe is to remember the <u>Gift of Life—</u>
To choose good or evil,
    remember FREEDOM—
If all of the choosing upon the earth
    is good, not evil:
We will walk in total freedom,
    for to choose evil is the
        surrendering of freedom, <u>our peace</u>,
our God-given right at birth.

9:56 AM    7/5/98

*Rosemary Regina Challoner Wilkinson*

# TO JAN SMREK  (1898-1982)

Now that I have come to know you,
    after honorably unveiling your portrait,
    still in memory/fastened to Writers House and my
    brain;
and having been born when your journalism
    and 'ELAN' gave birth to fame; I had to find
    your suffering, the silence, human view of woman,
    and love and life, so blessed and full.

I had to feel your deep depression of being
    removed, or walking in war, writing on the run,
    then rising to your feet, accomplishing so much
    in such short a time, even bestowing children's rhyme;
and I know all the great songs are written by men
    too, could be written from your pen, for while
    I toured your beloved Slovakia to the Low
    And High Tatra mountains, meadows so lush green:

No wonder you wrote love poems.
Yes, Slovienes have a special 'kind of mind'.

September 20, 1998
3:29 P.M.

World Congress of Poets/World Academy of Arts and
Culture
U.S.A.
(from visit of 18th WCP at Budmeirce, Slovakia)-Writers
House

## LIFE IS NOT

Life is not about success;
Life is about trials that
    you overcome.

                    10-4-98    9:13 A.M.
                    St. Francis feast day

## COME NORTH WITH ME

"Sing joyfully to the Lord, all you lands,
break into song, sing praise." Ps. 98


Come North with me to Oregon—
    let us explore their coasts, ours of California,
    through the "big trees of redwood", majestic, wind free,
    where a car travels through such width of old,
    come down from Foothills of mighty Sierras
    to Sacramento then west to Hartsook Inn
    where we spent our honeymoon October 15,
    fifty years ago in nineteen forty-nine.

Deep breathe the aroma of the pristine forest,
    preserved scant for posterity, see lights
    set low in window dining room affording
    rest and early walk along shores of winding
    Eel River, bending, curving, to cars delight
    where away from the concrete cities many flock
    to regain sanity, composure from fast-lane track.

To the North west on #101 to Oregon
    endowed with men who pour your gas,
    outstretched farms, old barns you yearn to paint,
    impeccable rows of black soil, still hiding produce
    to come, neat green/white houses, cattle nearby,
    or 'slow for crossing elk', blessed trees to ocean waves
    to Newport, fog horns, where ship's captain
    grandfather
    painted 'Yaquina Bay Harbor' in 1880's-1890's finally to
    become 19th Century Painters rave.


                October 12, 1998      11:51 A.M.

## LOVE IS BLIND

Love is blind like fog
which you cannot see
for it is ever-changing

11/7/98     11AM

# I WISH

I wish that I could remember
    the very first time that I closed my
        hands in prayer, closing my eyes,
to say a prayer, to feel God within
    my heart, and soul, leaving
        all round me to embrace heaven.

I wish that I could remember
    the very first time that I felt
        the Presence of God, in the
host on my tongue, tears in my eyes,
    thinking "I live now, not I, but
        Christ lives in me, through me."

           Nov. 18, 1998    9:17 A.M.

# HOW IS IT THAT WHEN

How is it that when God
    sets me aside, in bed, in pain,
        that I accept the rest, recovery
not questioning why, "what have I done?"
    but embracing the moment, to join
        my pain with His, on the Cross.

Then I can see His face bloody,
    experience His body throbbing,
        leaning forward with face
turned to the right, head of thorns,
    oozing drops of blood, excruciating pain,
        erasing all mankind's sins, dying
for each of us.

             Nov. 18, 1998    9:28 A.M.

# TANKA JOY

Cherry blossoms come
when cool spring stirs openly
to burst their birth bloom
and share such joyful wonder
so sacred into poem.

# SYNTHETIC TRUTH

Synthetic truth is a
       sickness, not
authentic, official,
       not truth.

Like lies it is a poison
       of sickness.

Time is the daughter
       of truth—take
a look of our record.

(find  1  Cor.  12/28/First:Apostles/Second:Prophets/Third:
Teachers—Mon Dieu!)

Dec. 10, 1998    4 PM

# POEM—"NOT A TREE"

Not a tree rising
    on the horizon
like Mississippi River
    on Highway #61...

                11 A.M.    Jan. 9, 1999

# JESUS

Jesus I see your love
    blooming in every flower
        falling with mountain streams;
I read of your cries in world hushed
    screams of the unborn
        begging to live, breathe.

Your voice is in the wind
    touching my back when praising
        you with tears from my heart.

When will you come to rescue
    your lost, abandoned and
        longing for your presence again?

        Jan. 21, 1999    8:23 P.M.

# CHERISHED 40 YEARS

When did these years go I so willingly
    gave with all devotion of caring, sharing
      and with fervor I entrusted all.

May they share with those yet coming forth
    this dedication that I leave for others
      so inspired the same.

May they remember most of all the perfection
    of Oriental Literature in action verbs
      and picture nouns uplifting our souls.

February 8, 1999    12:11 A.M.

# SPRING GREEN MOSS

Spring green moss erupts mid water flowing
    down enormous bold rocks along
        South Fork of the American River
near the Mosquito Road bridge where
    we pass under somber skies about to cry
        in Spring now-but winter
begging to stay-little while longer.

Look around to the daffodils blooming
    and hyacinths spreading their color
        to uplift our spirits from gray skies
reminding us of God's blessing to earth
    and all God created for human happiness in birth.

Let us praise the generosity mirroring heaven on earth.
Let us know that earth is of discovery, reward, mirth.
And in remembering we know fuller life, energy uplifting.

                March 24, 1999    3:14 P.M.

# THIS IS THE DAY OF THE LORD

Holy, holy, we bow down on this,
the day of the Lord, Sunday:
The day to write on the handmade
rice paper from Lokta plant
growing in Eastern Nepal
at 10,000 feet, gift
from Nepal poet, attending literary
meet with world poets, writers
from many nations to share
papers, poetry, culture,
traditions, heritage, literature
on precious soil of beloved
Valencia, Spain, cherished
by poets, authors, of old,
of present, and those to come, to walk
in their places continuing legacy
of eons ago, so cherished
a land, so blessed by God.

June 13, 1999     8:59 A.M.

# I SAW THIS TABLE

I saw this table and looked
for those behind it for cloth
came down in front, creasing
on each side into corner folds.

This I named a Sacred Table
for it turned into a square
Tabernacle, bright from sun,
Yet it appeared over TV.

What I was watching was EWTN
and 'Life of Ignatius of Loyola'
but the image over it
was what came from the sun.

I saw this table formed into Tabernacle
as plain as if I knelt before it,
praying in deep adulation,
feeling sacred, holy, countenance;

Was this table, the Last Supper, empty,
but filled Tabernacle to us replaced?
I asked, and the stark contrast
of new Presence great joy surpassed!

Saturday  8:05 P.M.   6/19/99

# THE MAN

The man with the
    furrowed face spoke
        to my soul, to my heart
in silence, with just a look,
    for with it the silence
        spoke to me of agony
and pain, a man in exile
    running from his
        beloved, sacred land
so desecrated by ethnic
    cleansing, brutality, violence
        and rape and murder
about one race, belief over
    another, leaving behind
        total destruction, hate,
killing of children in massive graves,
    and mindless, senseless belief,
        but God's tears filled the earth
to respond to justice the truth.

June 20, 1999
2:38 P.M.

# RAIN OF FALLING STARS

The stars of fire made by man
    fell over Washington, D.C.
        to celebrate two-hundred twenty-three
years of our U.S.A. history and as
    each rocket exploded rising to the sky
        it burst into expanding Universe
imaging lilies spreading arms so wide
    falling into, down, the East River
        of lower Manhattan too,
and Sacramento close to home,
    with Oregon too boasting same
        so America, coast to coast,
acclaimed 4$^{th}$ of July in all
    true pride and glory
        giving thanks to God
for our freedom of all peoples
    living on our land,
        safe refuge to so many
coming, staying, living, struggling again.

           July 5, 1999    8:39 P.M.

# BEHOLD ROMANIA
(dedicated to Ion Dumitru)


Blessed land of rich green forests,
    mountains rugged with tips of snow,
        and lakes, the Danube, flowers
exquisite in July for poets greeting
    many nations assembled in brotherhood
        coming, embracing from war-torn
lands in the sharing of poetry, Romania glory.

The Bishop of Curtea de Arges opened arms
    with Mayor explaining our coming in love, needing
        no translation, praying us into
further success "continue struggles of
    writing" feeling the pulse of nations
        and through translation filter down
into sharing a nations' culture, education.

So we feel the power, deep soul within
    a sacred land, close to God,
        many monasteries' prayers uplifting and
filling us with such rewarding devotion
    through priceless icons, candles lit,
        art of joy touching our soul
never to leave us as we leave this soil.

            July 17, 1999    4:04 P.M.

# THE LEPERS

I passed them by in 1986, sitting
    together on ground, up St. Thomas Road,
      Madras, India, and I did nothing.

Their dark, shrouded clothes hurt me
    to the core, hiding their sores, and I did
      nothing, walking up the steep hill.

How could I walk by fingering no bill
    but refraining from attention, love,
      a joining to listen, in a new friendship?

Do not emulate me, I did nothing.  I
    passed by, looking down, not stopping to pray
      or use talent, to encourage, from me.

How could I not cherish the moment, <u>do
    something</u>, or like Mother Teresa says,
      ask God permission to know, act, do?

It is written of talent given if not
    used will be withdrawn—and
      so by doing nothing—I passed by
and did nothing—do not emulate me.

               July 18, 1999     2:37 PM

# CAROLINA, PISCES FRIEND POET
### (Spirituality: No. 1  Industry-Romania)


Signs of wonder, awe in a tree, miracles
  of fish, snail, mole, spider, crocus, junipers,
    cherry blossoms, plum trees, sparrows
      and starlings: you bring alive to me.

How I too am drawn to Rilke, Emily, and add
  Donne, Teresa of Avila and John of the Cross,
    for your lyrical poetry of Transylvania reflects
      the same rising from the mundane material
        to a special feminine 'mysticism'.

Yes, we encounter the "whether, —whether not",
  for poetry seems not ours, but to own us,
    and in trepidation to risk our heart
      soul, mind and spirit to merge
        in a fast-end-product forthcoming.

Yes, we two wrote first poem at age fourteen,*
  though oceans removed, traveled nations,
    not comprehending the why of it all,
      part of children entering 3$^{rd}$ Millennium;
        you creating blessed land of Romania's
          Number One Industry: Spirituality.

*1$^{st}$ books of poetry 1973

July 18, 1999     4:16 P.M.

# OF LATE

Of late like a year
    now I sense the
        realness of Jesus's
right side above me
    on the Cross.

It always is alive
    to my right looking up
        sans Face and arms
for I am beneath them
    sensing a live presence,
at the time, just before
    He died.

                  8/1/99      5:53 P.M.

*Rosemary Regina Challoner Wilkinson*

# CHINA-10 YEARS LATER

Here in Beijing where dramatic change
   from cart-wheels to taxis, to cars
    and bicycles galore thrive
       every day from higher pay,

and the freeways replaced the wide
   streets but left the green, green trees
    and flowers bloom profusely
       lifting your heart and soul joyfully.

Here is where the China Radio International beams
   into many countries with China news
    and International TV is birthed
       spreading culture, traditions, unearthed.

See the cranes creating high-rises
   and replacing shacks with decks
       on tall apartments, restoring art
       in poetry, painting, music, calligraphy.

When last here, I saw Beijing as more
   beautiful than Paris, and now, I see
       modern Exhibition Hall welcoming nations
    and many hotels open to visitors.

Oh, Beijing, again, you steal my heart
   for your city is dressed out in new heartfelt art.

World Academy of Arts and
  Culture
World Congress of Poets

September 19, 1999
1:45 P.M.  Pacific
 Daylight Saving Time
U.S.A.

# PENGLAI, CHINA

Behold this city they call 'A Fairyland on Earth'
    beckoning world poets to witness birth
        of a literary meeting of old "in days of Li Po, Tu Fu"
            and eons of poets then spread at tables of
            wine.

Lo the city where China cherishes historical relics
    and Penglai Ge, famous world tower, fiery
        morning glows, warm sun rising at dawn,
            the splendor of moving clouds from deep blue
            sea.

Tombs of the Qis, Ming Dynasty Halls, Towers,
    heroes, corridors, grated cultural parks,
        flourishing flowers in land of quiet
            and respite thinking and praying.

Here where the flower fields reflect clouds
    floating about raising our hearts
        mingled with being removed
            yet in a city busy with work.

A pavilion watches the sea rise and flow
    to witness the reds and purples
        of the brilliant skies smiling down
            on a very special, special nation.

The exploding sun welcomes the world poets who
    will visit "Heaven Clear Palaces",
        "Stele Pavilion" of Favour and Kindness"
            and sleep in the evening glow of a setting sun.

*Rosemary Regina Challoner Wilkinson*

From such, much uplifting poetry will come.

September 19, 1999
2:13 P.M.
Pacific Daylight Saving Time

World Academy of Arts and Culture
World Congress of Poets

# ANGELS, WE LEARN

Angels, we learn are
　　helpers, while others
　　　　are sent to be felt; violent force
　　　　　　to flatten us hard to the ground.

The greatest physical power on earth,
　　I felt across my numb lower back
　　　　then the lifting of two, not one,
　　　　　　slowly upwards from me, one by one.

Who can fathom the mystery of life
　　knowing unseen spirits roam the earth,
　　　　some who come to heal, others hurt,
　　　　　　and some, through sin, actually devour.

Knowing God gives us appointed
　　ones, and others to call on for help,
　　　　and some to guide the Nations aright
　　　　　　into spreading rare peace upon the Earth.

　　　　　　　　9-27-99　　3:12 P.M.

# WITH MEXICO POETS-1999

They came from many nations
  to Acapulco in tropical sun
    with many colored faces
      and languages to match.
All these poets embraced each other
  in splendid harmony revealing
    souls of their beloved soils
      to exchange in new love as brothers.
The papers were read, poems recited, the
  applause and hugs by audience
    approved such a rarity
      forgetting negative, ideologies.
Warmth and loving generosity of Mexico
  welcomed the world poets, never
    to be forgotten: translations
      filtering down into education.
Youth of Mexico act out a poem,
  never mind the language, tell it
    so your eyes drip with emotion
      in poem revealing brother/sister
learning of his illness and told 'he
  would no longer be there
    when the leaves fall'; so she climbed the
      trees to sew leaves together...
Bravo, Mexico!  Fountainhead of Poetry.

        November 29, 1999
        2:15 P.M.

# FORGOTTEN GENERATION

When looking back to 60's forward
   we now see how they came along
      hilariously, to the rock-beat,
         of concerts and temptations.
Where were the educators teaching
   formal requireds unmindful of spirit,
      hidden deeply within, and too
         afraid to cry out from the pain?
Where were the religious who kept
   things "going on as usual" not hearing
      their plea in the rock music,
         only declaiming the same?
Did they not need to hear of abortion
   from condoms for the 'sexually active'
      education provided—youth accepted—
         only to learn one day—a lifetime away?
Think of thirty years later when this can change
   to give a new generation guide for the soul
      for heart never changes eager to learn
        to create a grateful generation
mindful of God.

               Rosemary C. Wilkinson, U.S.A.
               November 29, 1999  2:30 P.M.

# SR. RAPHAEL OF GOD LEFT US

Here, in the foothills of the
    mighty Sierra Nevada Mountains,
        where black oaks bereave the
            falling of gold leaves

we witness via satellite EWTN
    the hymns sung, the Word read,
        while bells peeled and procession
            followed, under somber heaven,

for the sky wants to cry as
    Mother Angelica bends to kiss
        this Raph (of God) for last time
            knowing only body is here

and spirit is with God, no longer
    to sing—her Panis and Ave Maria
        so our goose-pimple arms can feel
            the magic of her lofty voice

so we acquiesce and let her go—
    for she has another music chore now we know,
        but a tape here to hear her in delight
            asking her to pray for us

while waiting our turn to join with her, in Joyous
    Jubliee, mercy.

                    January 16, 2000  2:58 P.M.
                    U.S.A.

# BLESSED BE GOD
# BLESSED BE HIS NAME

The Lord took my hand—
led me into a wandering land
to see the planet where
only humans breathe;
to see the animals roaming ground,
fish in the waters, birds in air,
parents guarding their children
for in joy created them
and in a flash it was certainly clear
that what was temporarily here
was just a test knowing
right from wrong
to pass entrance into Eternity.
BLESSED BE GOD
BLESSED BE GOD'S NAME

Rosemary C. Wilkinson  1/18/2000  10:01 P.M.

# USE ME LORD

Let me know where it is you want me to go,
  whom to see, those avoid, let me know
    what it is that I can accomplish
      knowing I am doing as you will, with me;
I surrender my precious time left, to give it up,
  make room for important things, you want done,
    gathering poets from East, West, North, South
      to embrace as nations should in brotherhood.
Despite heavy work, family, reading, reviewing
  and meeting with Heads of State, despite
    time out for surgery, illness, trips and such
      I say yes, use me Lord, needing no response.
It seems I have done it all, went where you sent
  me, in complete faith, no explanation or why
    I packed the bags, left by jet, over and over
      Now nineteen times, for Congress of Poets.
When I look back over it you taught me, discipline
  through hospital administration, rearing four children,
    husband to acquiesce to it all, encouraging,
      standing by for arrival home, and just as
China in 2002 will accomplish great, after ten years wait,
  I know it must be all for some spiritual meaning
    that you keep gathering us poets from nations for
    peace.

March 4, 2000     7:57 P.M.

# NOTHING SACRED LEFT?

Where has "dignity and respect" in humans
      surrendered to what is "politically correct"
            or "self-esteem" raised egos to extreme
                  sans humility causing such to fail?
What causes "depression" to be the cop-out
      for not working whereby the Real Depression
            was men eating out of garbage cans coast
                  to coast, but especially in Chicago?
And rampant contagious "stress" causing
      relief in drugs, doctors visits, phony lies
            whereas when under stress best work
                  can come forth, erasing stress, deriving relief.
The many trials, tribulations of daily living
      are filled, compounded by computer addiction,
            TV, movies, disappearing children in street
                  to play off obesity—they die before forth-five.
Where will the arrogance of building this tower
      driven by power, greed, ignoring homeless,
            when some nations have little to eat
                  and others in opulence and plenty, choose
to ignore it all, deny God in education, proving
to the world, this culture of death, has nothing sacred left.

March 4, 2000      8:19 P.M.

# THERE IS A SOLUTION: THIRD MILLENNIUM

There is a solution to resolution of
    conflict and that is dialogue—
It is the only dire solution—war is
    obsolete—dialogue is the answer
for workable peace.

March 9, 2000    10:44 P.M.

# IT SEEMS I WAS

It seems that I was removed,
  and elevated upwards,
    knowing joy I never knew.

Then after some time I was
  displaced from elevation, lowered
    to another removal, midst the worldly throng.

It was here I wrote my best poetry
  between the swinging door of living
    with distraction I tried to understand.

But could not understand, but poetry,
  sustained me writing what was behest
    of me, and I studied, cherishing the best.

Yes, it seems, I never knew why the removals
  were both elevating and disciplined me
    to know aspects of life not found in books.

I found elevation and deflation so alike
  for it is part of my spiritual journey
    to present, when final call arrives.

To cherish those memories is precious to me,
  to live these moments again in privilege,
    to end life asking mercy, after all this, mercy.

Good Friday
April 21, 2000  7:34 P.M.

            Rosemary C. Wilkinson, U.S.A.

# WHILE I LISTEN TO HANDEL
(to someone who gave me strength)


While I listen to Handel, re-living "Alleluia",
I attend early Masses at St. Anne of the Sunset,
absorbing "Let Thy Hand Be strengthened" as I saw you
serving at foot of altar, in white over black, neath priest,
Denis James Mullen, now at rest, coming alive here before
us.

It was a holy time in life, when carefree, devoted to God,
not seeing through life's tunnel waiting ahead,
but just the scene present, living the moment,
not to comprehend the future turmoil of the world
or the part we would play on stage of life to unfurl.

We knew new feelings, not known heretofore, and
so alive pulsing, struggling to understand, while
watching with respect, dignity, in shyness, yes,
for a holy friendship is one we cannot talk of, or
surrender, if it is to be kept, holy, precious.

And so after sixty years of parting, praying, living
caught in web of a century's five wars
God chose the time, place, for holy embrace,
so the memory could live, clear, stand effaced
to know reality of life, unhidden God truly blessed.

May 22, 2000

# I BEHOLD THE FACE

I behold the Face of God
   in every rose that I see
      in every ship on the seas
         in every, and all of the trees.

I behold the Face of God
   in every human God made
      in every color of face
         in all nations' race.

I behold the very Face
   to teach me closeness of God
      in everything that I do
         in all things, my life too.

Where else can I go for this
   happiness I cherish deep in my heart
      in music, sacred art
         and in what I take part.

Blessed be the Face of God.

                May 26, 2000     1:19 P.M.

October 5, 2000

## All Holiness, Metropolitan Panteleimon II

From 30 years of 'devoted prelacy
    in the Apostolic Throne of Thessalonica'
        we world poets embraced XX WCP,
            Aug. 15-20, visiting St. Demetrius.

We saw your flower bouquets
    before Mary, cherishing your Icons,
        later seeing her on your gold chain
            close to your heart enshrined.

What precious, sacred soil, tread upon
    by Paul of Tarsus, many followers
        to birth history you carry on
            as you have filled us with love, devotion.

                        August 15, 2000
(What a great joy to turn on TV and see your services while there!)

Thank you and asking your blessing on our Academy,

# HOLY THESSALONIKI, 2000 A.D.

Here in Agios Demitrius, 5th Century Church
    where world poets come to embrace; we come
to walk where Paul walked, talked and from
    such encounters Christianity took birth, flourished.
Demetrius born 3rd Century, martyred by Galerius,
    later caused enemy to flee, appearing in sieges as
war-like warrior, later miracles performing.
Josephus (38-100 BC) wrote of Delos, Aegean island
    synagogues, where 'well formed marble benches,'
    center
of which is splendid marble 'throne' recalling
    "Seat of Moses" as found at Chorazin and Hammath-
    Tiberias.
In 1900 some 80,000 Jews lived in Thessaloniki with 30
synagogues,
    ten clubs, 4 high schools, 15 grade schools, college;
    54,000 wiped out
from Greek Holocaust, destruction, properties lost, now
1200 identify with past.
Thessaloniki, in former days, poet Samuel Ushkue called:
    "Metropolis" of Israel, cit of Justice, mother of Israel,
    like
holy Jerusalem.    Today marble Menorha Monument of
perished from
    holy shores of memory would cause Alexander the
    Great
to weep, from such intense grief, shed his tears over-
flowing
    into rivulets down into the Aegean sea, weeping,
Yes, weeping, flowing, flowing down, into the Aegean Sea.

Nathaniel Bartholomew would join him, year after year,
    in whom there is found no guile, O Israelite, add our
    tears,
        fill the Aegean with our sorrow, weeping
            weeping, weeping, weeping, not later, by 50
            years.

                August 24, 2000  11:55 A.M.
                Feast St. Bartholomew, Nataniel (72 AD)

# IN THESSALONIKI "HALKIDIKI"

In Thessaloniki near the Aegean sea,
   I am under the ripe olive tree,
      while the world poets gather
         to rest in the sand, swim in this bay.

Yes, swim and sing and dance to the romance
   of the warm blue water, swaying breeze,
      fluttering the leaves, joining all this happy
         East meeting West, through poetry.

Where else more fitting, more proper than this,
   that it should take place in sacred Greece,
      whose tradition and history form into one,
         and open their arms to all nations' poetry.

Your philosophers, poets and saints of old,
   join us here, smile down, welcome us, pleased
      with such success joyfully, one with us—
         Noble Greece, truly indeed, you are in our
         hearts.

               August 24, 2000   12:16 P.M.

# WEEKS OF AUGUST 14-26, 2000 XX WCP-GREECE

It is not accident we arrive in Thessaloniki,
sleepy, tired, feast of Maximilian Kolbe,
patron of Printers, Publishers (1894-1941), martyred
in WWII, but we come pleading publishers,
to open their doors, to world poets, print their work.

The nations gather to read papers, recite poetry,
visit cultural, artistic, archeological sites,
boating on Aegean, book sharing exchange, raising spirits.
Many translations will follow this historical
gathering, filtering down into worldwide educational
systems.

Between all this each day heaven celebrates
Mary's Dormition, Stephen of Hungary, Hyacinth
of 13th Century, Helena, patroness of converts, difficult
marriages,
founder of the True Cross, John Eudes, Founder
Charity nuns,
to help prostitutes, and Bernard of Clairvaux, Founder of
Benedictines.

Even Pius X, Lady of Knock, Queenship of Mary, Rose of
Lima,
    patroness of South America, Bartholomew, King Louis
    of France,
Patron of Tertiaries, and birthday of Mother Teresa of
Calcutta,
    so many, many more, as heaven is one with us,
as nations' poets join to uplift all of mankind.
Rise up poets! Write, recite, Spread your work abroad
Leave something behind so they know you were here.

                August 24, 2000   12:45 P.M.

# WITH POETS IN THESSALONIKI

Here where Paul, walked and talked, after
Josephus (38-100 B.C.) told of Delos, Aegean island
of the synagogue where well-formed marble
benches,
center with 'marble throne', recalling "Seat of
Moses"
as found at Chorazin and Hammoth-Tiberias.

In 1900 some 80,000 Jews lived in Thessaloniki with
thirty synagogues, ten clubs, college, four high schools,
fifteen grade schools almost totally wiped out from
Green Holocaust, synagogues destroyed,
properties lost,
and today 1,200 partake of history, help retain identity with
past.

Thessaloniki, of former days poet, Samuel Ushkue,
titled this sacred soil "metropolis" of Israel, city of
Justice, mother of Israel, "like Jerusalem" and
Alexander the Great would keel, kneel indeed,
at the
Menorrha monument "54,000 Jews of her perishing" from
Holocaust.

August 26, 2000   3 P.M.

# GREATEST BIO EVER WRITTEN

It seems that when I awake
　　in early morn, and finger
　　　　my Rosary through fifteen
　　　　　　decades, I feel a calm,
not obtained any place, on face of earth.

The first five tell me of the
　　announcing to Mary of Jesus' birth,
　　　　second, her visit to cousin Elizabeth,
　　　　　　third of shepherds adoring in Bethlehem,
fourth presenting him, finding him in holy Temple

The second five tell me of his agony in the garden,
　　next scourging him by Pilate, Roman soldiers
　　　　crowning him with thorns, people watching
　　　　　　him drag, fall, stumbling to Calvary
where Jesus died for every one of us born.

It was told he descended into Hell, appeared
　　to nations round the world, arose from the dead,
　　　　ascended to Heaven bodily, sent Holy Spirit
　　　　　　of love, to empower men, and Mary too,
assumed into Heaven and proclaimed our Queen:

Do I see her as Queen of Heaven, Earth, Poetry,
　　yes, and feel all unrestlessness in my heart
　　　　vanish as I finger every bead, for my need,
　　　　　　and my spirit, demeanor turn quiet, calm
to face the day, erase my way, to do God's will.

　　　　　　　　Sept. 9, 2000  9 A.M.

# AT BEPOE BAY, OREGON

O grandeur, magnificence of God
    in all these clashing waves
        against the ocean rocks
and white foam returning, to sea
    while sun kisses in glistening
        peaks the blue green
water in a rhythm rare but
    full of welcome sound
        lifting my spirit anew.

How I love the blue sky
    meeting far horizon away
        and the air is clean to breathe
from back home and the hot sun
    here where so many come to
        cool and rest away
from it all taking time out
    to remember difference between
        material and spiritual gain.
Yes, here where the heart speaks to God.

        September 17, 2000
        4:06 P.M.

# THE "SPOTLESS ONE"

"All generations shall call me blessed"
He has raised the lowly to high places
He has promised his Mercy to Israel
And to us through the birth of Jesus Christ
He has given us salvation to spend all eternity
At the end of 'time' where there is Eternal happiness
And glory to God by all nations
By those gathered from each generation
Generation, generation, generation.

October 2, 2000    8:45 A.M.

# PASSING BY OF A SAINT (1938-San Francisco)

We are in uniforms from
    St. Ann's School in San Francisco
      lining the stairs up to the
Cathedral of St. Mary's on the hill
    for the Pope Pius XII was
      rising step by step from car
    below on the crowded street
      watching him as we watched
        him coming closer until
he was right next to me looking
    into his gaunt face and
      colorful robes but most of all
I remember seeing his turned-up-
    toe-purple shoes which my eyes
      could not leave pass by
and I wanted never to leave there
    as this saint turned his head
      and I bowed mine at age fourteen.

October 23, 2000
9:59 P.M.

(Pius XII when Cardinal)

## "THE WINDS"

The winds were all strong,
swirling round tall pines at night,
next morn earthquake struck
shaking our beds, scaring hearts,
new shake, not like all before.

7:36 A.M. (tremor 4.9 Richter) Dec. 2, 2000
(foothills of mighty Sierra Nevada Mountains)

# IT HAPPENED IN CHINA

It came from diligent work
    envisioned by one man from China,
        a woman from U.S.A. to
present the world with "POETRY PEACE ANTHOLOGY"
by U.N. HEADS OF STATE never, ever done before.

The poems, statements, with photo
    stretched across two wide pages
        translated into six languages
on slick, 1000 hard-back cover, and
1,000 new silk-technology never, ever used before.

These words from leaders of nations
    reveal the spirit uplifting mankind
        we all yearn to see fulfilled
to bring our nations to respect each other
and love as human sisters and brothers should.

Yes, we turn in space as a global village,
    from many cultures, beliefs, color, race
        all spinning on one planet moved by heaven
to live here on earth, as those already gone,
perfecting our way of exchange through knowledge,
peace.

We yearn for this all to come about now:
These "Messages" give us that bright, new hope.

                    Dec. 8, 2000  8:13 P.M.

# IN BEIJING, AGAIN

Ten years later China is a bustling
    nation with tall cranes building
        living and business, and industry
exploding on the scene with expressways
and taxi's like New York or London or Paris.

Walking along the wide mall where
    no cars move and flowers bloom aglore
        attractive windows draw us to shop
and vendors sell their wares, here and there,
where I buy sweaters and incense to burn.

The wind blows our winter clothes
    and we push hats down not to fly
        walking near water at the Summer Palace
and dreaming for the snow to fall on ground,
when back at San Francisco, resting by a fire
in joyful memory of China leading all nations
forth to rise up and restore our pure poetry.

December 8, 2000    8:35 P.M.

# WINTER TANKA

Snow melts, water fills
the Sacramento River,
lakes, along the way,
flowing down from our foothills
through the "Gate" to sea.

Dec. 12, 2000     10 AM

# THOSE WHO "CAN DO"

Those who are the 'can do'
        draw others to follow
            'can do' too.

Blessed be the leaders
        who inspire the followers
            to 'can do'
to 'get it all done'.

December 25, 2000
3:31 P.M.

# THE FUNERAL

And so, from first breath of life
    to the last here on earth,
        the next is our first in heaven
where peace surrounds us and
    no further tears of pain is found:
        we know our destiny is over.

With first breath came our time
    for living, eating, sleeping
        to reach, search for coming,
as the mind and body matured
    leaning more and more each day
        for purpose given by heart and heaven.

All the years we toiled, following one
    after another, facing distractions, failure
        and success lead us forward
reaching upward to seventy and over
    when time out came to rest, enjoy
        the past, recall all fulfilled purpose.

Time arrives to breathe our last,
    content to see it come, prepare to go,
        read and pray, so much time,
seems to pass, happy with all accomplished,
    from way back to first breath taken
        to our next, the last, ready now to breathe heaven.

           December 25, 2000
           7:31 P.M.

# SAY A PRAYER
## (departing Beijing)


When in line of departure for
    those flying with you
        beginning with the agent
checking you in, cart-man
    assisting your luggage to
        counter within, all those
rushing by finding their way
    and the vendors duty-free ware
        plus the ones pushing brooms
or handing your change from tea
    you will sip while planes
        arrive, depart to their port
but most of all say a prayer
    for your captain, his crew,
        those who serve you or
speak/or not in your language,
    those who unload, or luggage
        find, if lost.
Say a prayer when you rise upwards
as the 'angels lift your wings' as prayer does.

                January 7, 2001   3:50 P.M.

# WE HUNG HIM NAKED

We hung him naked,
    no, not the Jews, Roman soldiers,
        we hung him naked, we:
the world, no one else, no one else.

Did it happen and end back then,
    no, we all do it over, over again,
        in every way, by what we say, or through
disrespect, and even pretend.

His name is used in horror, shock,
    in rage, disappointment, unbelief
        in movies, TV, by teens, the old
by any, everyone, unbowed heads, bold.

We do it by money and power and war
    in hatred of each other, unkind deeds,
        making atom bombs, missiles to kill another
never mindful that each act drips blood from his fingers.

So when will we learn to change, nations change,
    use resources to feed hungry, house homeless,
        serve medicine, education to earth's children
or just go on hanging him, bleeding more blood
as we behold him dying over and over for us
every day we live, dying with him until our end.

Jan. 14, 2001     5:31 P.M.

# IN THE WOODS
## (EL DORADO FOREST)

Come with me to walk here,
    behold the vast forest of trees
        some dripping with green-gray moss,
          some old, and craggy,
as the fresh wind powders our face.

Come, let us walk slowly where
    dust and pebbles which we sway to miss
        and see even some apple trees
          planted years ago, strive
to live, from Spring blossoms to Fall.

What is it about a forest and you alone
    want to feel together the quiet we seek
        from hurried lives and speak-speak
          to place us into the sacred and holy
of planet earth, among, between, all that is old.

What a joy it is to feel all of this—
Privileged feeling God gives to us,
Recalling "I the Lord have created it."*

*Isaiah 45:8          Rosemary C. Wilkinson, U.S.A.
                    April 1, 2001  2:42 P.M.

# FEELINGS ARE THESE

What are these feelings that I feel
   when beholding this man, head bowed,
      hat clutched in hand, kneeling alone
         on the floor as passers go by in hurry.
and inside me I watch closely the man crying.

He kneels in back of church on bare floor
   so intent in his thoughts rushing here, there
      and everywhere as he feels compassion far
         from the cross up front stretched wide
with pain, looking down to the right, sorrowful.

Flowers grace both these sides bright, candles behind:
Both these remind me of one dying, rest of us pardoned.

                Holy Week  Apr. 8, 2001  4:50 P.M.

# GREATEST BOOK EVER WRITTEN

I walked in the Garden Gethsemane
    mid the knarled ancient olive trees
        spreading a blushing-gray upon the agony
            reminding us of the blood dripping from
            knowing,
what is to come, feeling the drips down, one by one.

Next came flashing of lashes sounding,
    resounding down through the centuries, down
        through us, hearing strikes blow over and over
            breaking the flesh, dripping precious blood and
open wounds continue to open, drip blood, heavier thereof.

The thorn crown, pressed mightily down
    with the might of Roman soldiers strength
        and each thorn erupting, spouting fresh new blood
            to all this sorrow, crying we feel,
amid the mocking, insults, cruelty back then.

This thirty-three old was chosen over 'a guilty'
    to die, after the washing of Roman hands,
        goaded by Roman soldiers up rocky hill Calvary,
            nailed to a wooden cross, we kiss as we pray,
remembering all this happening, over and over again.

Lastly we look up at a naked shining sweat body,
    from full bloom of life, human but divine,
        that difference from us, knees bent, flesh gone,
            open red flesh pierced right side, limbs wide:
all to remind us every wrong we commit, world commits,
bleeds this sacred body, through love, atoning for us.

We are not to look for Rome soldiers, leaders,

people of Chosen Israel, but a promise fulfilled
to errant mankind since Time began
and to search our own hearts
to learn the joy, we partake in, our rising to Heaven.
Why?  because God wants everyone saved.
God wants every nation saved.  Alleluia.

May 10, 2001  8:53 A.M.

# ENROUTE TO LEAVENWORTH
(Washington, U.S.A., that is)


Behold the majesty of such gigantic Cascades
    peaking with snow melting to meadows below
        and tall pine trees dressed out in eloquence
        with snow still piled aside the road
dripping our drinking water so clear, pure, to behold.

What magnificence of all this purity, God's gift
    to absorb away from bustle of it all,
        deep breathe here, never wanting to let go,
            never  leave  its  Wenatchee  River  flowing
            through
or just keep it cherished in our hearts and
    later on share with God.

                May 10, 2001
                11:32 A.M.

*Rosemary Regina Challoner Wilkinson*

# WASHINGTON (U.S.A.) TO CALIFORNIA

See the twisting Sacramento River, blazing along
    yellow scotch broom, deep green grass, azaleas,
        rhodendrons, strong disciplined pines
            reaching arms to embrace you, and light
spring-green aspens, later birches, some still dripping
cones.

In Oregon a solid mass of white cloud,
    shape of gigantic space ship, nose and all,
        floats following us over Mt. Shasta,
            over one mass of solid pine trees as
far as eye can see, raising both sides en masse.

Mountains surround us of enormous elevations,
    dwarfing us and rolling cars down the hill,
        dropping elevation to 2,000 where borders
            of Oregon and California kiss together the
blooming poppies along freeway I-5.

Many trucks flash past disappearing towns, ranches,
    steer, cows, sheep, 'chain-up-signs' for skiers,
        as down, down we go, past Sacramento,
            and sixty miles more to our home,
now 78° on car, along curving roads to Placerville
village of the Foothills of the mighty Sierra Mountains.

                        May 12, 2001  8 P.M.

# STAY THE COURSE

In background a choir sings,
　　white/red robed young, open wide
　　　　to the music, so solemn, so holy.

Outside the hundred feet pines drip
　　new light-green cones to soon fall
　　　　and petunias, sweet peas, roses,
　　　　　　azaleas all bloom in full glory.

Where the temperature will rise to 103° in
　　Sacramento and Delta breeze coming
　　　　through Golden Gate slot will rise
　　　　　　to cool us here at 3,000 feet.

All this reminds me of how nature
　　is governed by God in rising, setting of sun,
　　　　and nature "stays the course", a
reassurance of us to 'stay the course', be at peace.
Sometimes a step into conflict is to resolve peace.

　　　　　　　　May 20, 2001  10:45 A.M.

# THE NATURAL LAW

Resting, after long week of pressing work,
    a TV expert spoke only a few words to me.
        First he said Moses given right, wrong
            to follow: not to hurt anyone or
steal, lie, adultery, kill, obey God.

We know right, wrong in our heart
    from conscience at birth,
        as the natural law guides us
            to listen, do right, not wrong.

We know in our heart when we do wrong,
    which we call God's love coming alive,
        to live in us, to awaken us more
            the right to choose, right from wrong,
to live in peace after the right choosing given to us by God.
Will we 'decision' suffer, yes, but choosing right brings
peace.

                    May 20, 2001  10:58 A.M.

Poet OVID: Met.7:19 Translation: "I see the better things
and I approve of them, but I pursue the worse things."

# CALM AT DAWN

As only light appears
    before the sun, and
        the wind is calm,
            even time lies quiet,
for time to think, rest or prayer.

There is something here to cherish
    after awakening in morn,
        freedom not to stir,
            but to feel all alone, the stillness,
before hurried space of day.

How refreshing it is to deep
    sleep the tired body at night
        with the moon slowly rising
            beckoning us, calming us,
quieting us, from our harried, tired day.

The refreshing awakening is taking time to wonder
    of the blessing of doing each as we ponder
        how many who have gone before us would
come back to this same old quiet calm.

                May 26, 2001  3:37 P.M.

# THE GLORY AND OURS

And so the Glory came on a Sunday morn
    when the empty tomb beckoned us to come,
        look, and believe it empty, but a joy
           filled us we could not explain
but just stand and absorb it all, over, again.

Another forty days would pass while future
    plans were laid to carry on the Last Supper,
        in the Mass said round the world today,
           so we never forget the work of Father in Son:
"Do this in Commemoration of Me" until end of Time.

Yet another ten days pass when a promise made
    exploded in the wind gifting of Spirit as was told
        upon twelve holy apostles, 120 disciples, Mary,
           Mother of God as she called herself in Mexico,
and the people round about heard them all speak in
tongues.

About thirty years later, Mary was assumed,
    called the Dormition, into Heaven to join
        all those apostles, disciples, who spread the Word
           that Jesus was truly the Messiah, Holy One,
who came to earth to die, at thirty-three, for all world sins.

In Heaven Mary was crowned "Queen" to reign
    forever with Jesus, the King, under our Father,
        along with all the saints and angels, even us,
           doing God's will here on earth,
as God does every moment that we live here, and in
Heaven.

June 3, 2001  4:07 P.M.

# GLORY OF HEAVEN ON EARTH

Look, look at heaven blessing the earth
    every tree greening its leaves—
        every flower shedding in a bower—
            of delight and joy every day, all day long.

See the ocean, seas, and gulfs
    rushing our blessed waters forth
        so we live in happiness, contained,
            all the day long through, every single day.

What magnificence from flying over clouds
    below us, men in space to show
        us, our globe spinning round, until
            the end of Time, as we know time, by God.

Yes, earth reflects the heavenly peace
    we share together as nations become brothers,
        obsoleting war, all people sharing
            food, housing, medication, education,
and fulfillment of happiness knowing all this;
for we are no longer blind, but resigned to will of God.

                July 20, 2001  8:31 A.M.

# WHEREFORTH SHALL WE GO?

In centuries up to 19$^{th}$ we have slavery
    and serfdom, caste systems, and so forth
        until 20$^{th}$ when holocaust, ethnic
            cleansing rose up and now in 21$^{st}$
abortions, AIDS, run rampant, the wide world over.

Coming to our attention is "Roe vs Wade"-1973
    when Supreme Court declared legal for all the
        nine months; 2000 declared "ban on
            partial birth abortion" un-constitutional
and recently "all babies are humans".

Back to Isaiah "Woe to those to call evil good
    and good will, evil; who put darkness for light
        and light for darkness, (like California, of late)
            or bitter for sweet, sweet for bitter"
and busy world, in a hurry, to know our fate?

June 24, 2001
2:38 P.M.

# REST, PRAY, WHILE SET ASIDE

It is time out for being removed
    from the hurried world, time to read,
        and think of this other world
            of quiet, repose, body lying still.

It is time to enjoy no daily routine
    but simply to rest, recover surgery,
        and pray for so much rushing
            the mind, mostly for giving thanks.

It is time to feel others, needed by you,
    not you, needed by them, and
        time to plan things you always
            wanted to do when well again.

So while each day the body rests
    the mind, when pain is gone, races
        to accomplishments planned to do
            when up and well all over again.
What precious time to give God thanks
For all we are given, down or up, daily to us.

(and husband earning
degree in housewifery)        August 3, 2001
                         11:10 A.M.

# MORNING PRAYER

Holy heavenly Father, we thank you
for the night's rest, and this food,
we are about to eat

Asking you to bless us, our children,
their children, all of our relations
living or deceased, or among

The holy souls waiting to enter the
Kingdom of God, for all those
sick, suffering, in agony

And about to die now, or
all day long today, or
those who committed suicide

With no one to pray for them,
or committing suicide now,
or abortion, now, all day long

For God wants everyone saved
God wants every nation saved. Amen. Alleluia.

August 3, 2001    11:30 A.M.

# WORLD CONGRESS OF POETS

Satan has sifted me like
    wheat since 1973
        when I joined the world
            poets who write of beauty,
love, truth, and justice in joy.
Are we like two sides of
    one coin teaching us of truth,
        but I ask to be taught
            such with love
in confidence, fearless assurance?
We grew each year, why
    we do not know, as if
        heaven deemed it so,
            and a family of lowly poets
left solitary garrets to uplift the world, anew.
In thirty-two years, twenty-one
    nations opened their hearts, arms to
        welcome the multi-colored faces,
            all languages, professions,
for what poet earns a living as poet today?
Nations are in line to the year 2013
    to newer lands, newer cultures, uplifting
        a brotherhood of nations, calling
            for dialogue, making war obsolete,
so a new earth reigns in peace, in love.

August 14, 2001   10:22 P.M.

# TEARS OF WATER, TEARS OF BLOOD

While the world turns round,
   dripping tears, called love,
      are shedding for us, where
         these drip into healings,
and miracles are being embraced.

Look to Bolivia, Mexico, Japan, Croatia
   and Africa, Venezuela, Italy,
      Belgium, the U.S.A. and Sicily,
         many, many messages calling us
"return to God", prevent chastisement.

Science is baffled unable to comprehend
   sweet fragrance of stigmata but confirm
      the DNA present in the human blood;
         we recalling "no time to repent" flowed the
         flood,
now time to turn our lives over to God?

Reform, hear call to purity, holiness to God, weeps
   Mary, not flood, but fire from heaven,
      will come, cries Mother of all humanity, Jesus
         who died for all mankind, who loves
us, warns us, hope for a second chance?

Look around: Jesus is dripping the blood, Mary the tears.

               August 16, 2001
               8:47 P.M.

# ENROUTE TO PLACERVILLE

This curvy, scenic, switch-back
   road, winds down into town
      without yellow lines, and
         all driving "yield to uphill",
go slow, to cross one-way bridge.

Every, or any day, to town is like a
   drive through the country
      feasting on wild blooming flowers
         or strong green ferns which die
in freezing winter, rise up in spring.

Spring brings cascading water falls
   down rugged rocky hills from snow
      melting, dripping, falling,
         from on high hills down into South
Fork of American River flowing, flowing down,
   through Sacramento, under Golden Gate bridge
      as Pacific Ocean blesses the welcome
      water with sunsets galore.

               Aug. 30, 2001 8:28 P.M.

# THIS IS HOW

This how it used to be:
    the Tabernacle of Gold recessed
        behind the Altar Table, sided by flowers
            endowed, with red hanging candle
blinking us welcome, come to pray, rest.

Yes, this is the way, and new
    confessionals now, to use, more added,-
        plus new stained-glass inspiring
            windows-arousing special deep joy,
as we walk on carpet, statues admire.

These are changes stirring cherished
    memories of girlhood, recalling
        baptism, confirmation, marriage
            ceremonies, holy processions, holy ways,
holy days, hours before Blessed Sacrament.

All of hymns we grew up with, and
    learned by heart, Stations of Cross,
        first given to us by Mother Mary, Rosaries,
coming alive daily no matter where we are,
    living in my heart again.

                    August 30, 2001  8:42 P.M.

# THE NEW YORK FIRE PLANE

The perfect hit burst into sky flames
    piercing my brain three thousand miles away,
        then went farther past my hills dripping my tears,
            into the ocean past the Golden Gate, so
I could erase heart pain, never leaving me now.
It was 9 A.M. back east, everyone at work
    in two high-rises, separately hit and
        6 A.M. here, while I am praying my daily
            three Rosaries for the sick, suffering
those in agony, those about to die, then, all day long.
But since Tuesday September 11, 2001, my fingers
    move as if they know not what I know
        by heart, for I keep re-running the two
planes bursting over and over in my brain.
What is this I want to forget, never replay,
    never see the rubble, steel, blinding dust
        falling over burned, crushed bodies
who once sang, laughed, loved, children embraced.
I knelt down with those kneeling, crying
    in the rain, churches in ceremonies to
        hear the Imam, Rabbi, Christians, and Billy
        Graham,
whose words melted our souls deep with them in ground.
O God, fill our pierced heart from a ball of fire; play
    me the Panis Angelicus; lift our arms
        to the blue sky again, and red setting sun,
so America can live in peace once more again.
Assuage our depression with our national prayer
For God wants everyone saved, every nation saved.

                    September 15, 2001  9 P.M.

# WHO WILL COME

Who will come
  before me
  to keep company
  with me at the Cross?


Who will come
  before me
  to go among the poor
  and live with them?


Who will come
  before me
  to visit the sick,
  prisoners, those on death row?


Who will come
  before me
  to gather the young
  worldwide to uplift humanity?


Who will come to embrace third
    millenium to God into the new
    Kingdom God prepares for us--
All those who come to God.


September 19 1998  5:50 P.M.

# EPILOGUE

*Rosemary Regina Challoner Wilkinson is one of the great poets, mystics, and peacemakers of modern times. The list of her many activities, achievements, and awards, attests to her uniqueness and prophetic role in our world.*

*Rosemary is a person of deep spirituality, creative mind, and compassionate heart. Her poetry, reflecting her message of universal brotherhood, peace, justice, non-violence, love and truth, is well known for its depth as well as its simplicity. Only an articulate intuitive genius can blend this kind of depth and simplicity. She does it harmoniously and successfully.*

*When I say she can blend depth and simplicity, I am talking about a special dimension of inner discipline and mystical experience, a certain integrity and personal growth, a warmth and openness to others and to things, which are a fertile ground for fruitful action. Without this profound human understanding, love will tend to be deceptive, and poetry superficial. Rosemary's pen invites the reader to become aware of the fact that one cannot become perfectly human until one becomes partly divine. This is why her dedication to world peace is conceived through the inner life of the spirit. This is why her journey across religious traditions, cultures, countries, and disciplines, makes her a woman of international recognition, driven by the power and magic of creativity.*

*Directly or indirectly, Rosemary reveals her true vision of how to understand the language of God as expressed especially in nature and in the love for one another. She is blessed for knowing and carrying out her responsibilities toward humankind. She works very hard at not disappointing anyone and especially the "ONE" who generously gave her so many talents. And she lovingly and intelligently invests her talents and they keep growing.*

*What Rosemary writes is at once poetic, profound, yet clear and practical. When readers finish reading a poem of hers, they find they want to go back and study each sentence and each word, then start a new way of thinking and living. In reading her words, one's feeling is not only, "I see," but also, "I must do it." True leaders possess the secret of combining authoritative teachings with effective motivation by relating what they have to say to everyday life. Even though poetry seems transcendent, psalm-like, a cosmic song, it remains, however, firmly attached to the things of this world. Rosemary's words have this precious quality of attracting the reader to her vision of wholeness and fullness of life, while dealing with the problems, anxieties, and violence of our times. "Wisdom found in poetry," she wrote, "is our only substitute for modern warfare" (Poetry: Nature, p. 56). Isn't this remarkable!*

*Although most of Rosemary's poems are short and spare, they are to the point. In a few words, she says volumes. She emphasizes content more than structure. She doesn't see a problem between content and formality. For her, it is the fire which allows the hearth to be built, not the other way around.*

*In our modern days which show antagonism to poetry, Rosemary dares to use her poetic talents to convey her humanistic vision of peace, love, freedom, and reconciliation. "To speak of poetry today," she wrote, is to praise God and to serve all humankind." (Poetry: Nature, 57)*

Rosemary is leading a quiet and gentle revolution in poetry, in the peace process, and in human development. Her message is brilliant and prophetic. She wants us to understand the meaning of human existence and to live the fullest and noblest life.

Aren't we very close to such poetry of Rosemary Wilkinson when we read her work and her invitation "when you light a candle think of me"? Is not our special calling to this earth like the flower's calling?    When the flower blooms, it is spring everywhere, indeed.    Rosemary is in tune with whom they call 'blessed are the peacemakers'. Read her work with great interest and joy.

**Jean Maalouf, Ph.D.**
Author-U.S.A.

# EPILOGUE II:

There is no greater challenge today than bringing people and poets from different cultures to meet at yearly congresses-"W.C.P.'s" in various countries, and to raise their voice's in unity for 'World peace!'

Rosemary has succeeded to do this for 30 years, with all her heart, all her soul, and expertise. She has through devotion, commitment and love of humankind, created an international family of poets—who all love her, admire and thank her warmly for giving us and the world—this precious gift...

May the SING IN THE WIND WITH LOVE become a harmonious philarmony ringing its bells of peace and love all over the global village, bathed in Rosemary's glowing eyes and angelic smile...

**Ada Aharoni**, Ph.D. (ISRAEL)
Vice President-World Congress of Poets/World Academy Arts/Culture

# About the Author

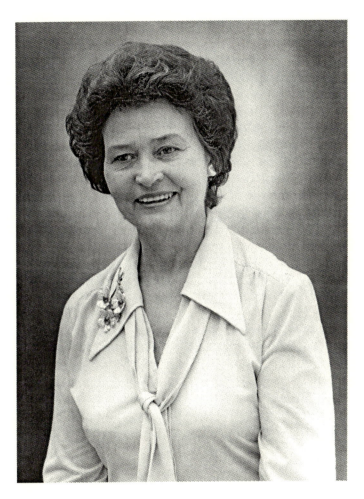

**Photo by Nancy Frank, San Mateo, CA**

The author is presently serving world poets as President World Academy of Arts and Culture convening World Congress of Poets held under auspices of the

Academy since 1973. She has attended all of these except first in 1969 and served a Sec. Gen. During 1985-1995 and as President 1994-2003

She is the author of 20 books of poetry, some poetry of which is translated into 36 languages, latest title POETRY: SPIRITUAL. Her prose works include AN HISTORICAL EPIC re WWII inside the U.S.A., serially translated into Mandarin Chinese and published in *NEW LITERATURE* in Taipei, China. The other prose work is the biography titled: *EPIC OF THE SHIP'S CAPTAIN/ARTIST* who was a 19th Century Painter and she wants to bring him forward to take his rightful place among the 19th Century Painters for little is known of him. She did an original research of twelve years, finding more than 42 of his paintings, 7 of which are on permanent exhibit in Louisiana State Museum in New Orleans where he shipped out of during exploding banana trade with Belize. He earned his 1st/2nd Mates from Her Majesty the Queen of England then Master's of OCEANS/SEAS/GULFS from the U.S.A. being citizen thereof. Wilkinson presently writes her autobiography *POET: UPLIFT MANKIND* derived from her 38 year literary career, having served prior to that in 10 years of hospital administration, rearing four children in 34 years. Her leadership for poetry is to bring forth poets in the world to their proper place in society for the poet is the soul of the nation he/she cherishes when revealing such sacred soil to other nations. Future generations will come to know their own beloved nation through a poet's eyes and heart and soul.

Printed in the United States
87066LV00001B/310-399/A

9 780759 669512